Borderline Failure:
National Guard on the Mexican Border, 1916-1917

A Monograph
by
MAJ Brent A. Orr
U.S. Army, NCARNG

School of Advanced Military Studies
United States Army Command and General Staff College
Fort Leavenworth, Kansas

AY 2011

Abstract

Borderline Failure: National Guard on the Mexican Border, 1916-1917 by MAJ Brent A. Orr, USARNG, 54 pages.

When President Woodrow Wilson ordered approximately 150,000 National Guardsmen to the southern border in 1916, the United States was on the verge of all-out war with Mexico. The rapid mobilization and deployment of the Guard forces broke the rapid escalation of violence, averted immediate war, changed the environment, and were instrumental in shifting the initiative, tactically and diplomatically, back to the Americans. Although there was no decisive victory by General John J. Pershing's punitive expedition deep inside Mexico and the National Guard struggled to meet the War Department's division-level collective readiness expectations, their ability and commitment to mobilizing quickly resulted in termination of the conflict on terms favorable to the United States.

While reviewing literature on this topic, two common themes emerged. The first was that few writers have written, in any depth, regarding the operational and strategic impact of the National Guard's 150,000 soldier deployment to the border. The second is that few writers attribute the termination of hostilities to that deployment.

This paper reviews President Wilson's actions and misunderstanding of the problem. It also briefly describes how the National Guard (organized militia) evolved very quickly. And finally it attempts to cast a different light on the Pershing Punitive Expedition to illustrate how this action inadvertently incriminated the environment and escalated tensions to near all-out war.

Amidst war plans which lacked substance for mass mobilization, an extremely short time-line, toxic rhetoric from preparedness-movement advocates, and confusion about their new role under the Defense Act of 1916, the citizen soldiers got to the border quickly and changed the dynamics of the environment. It was not a decisive victory but Wilson understood it was good enough.

Table of Contents

Introduction

The United States National Guard entered a critical point in history for its growth,

modernization, and legitimacy between 1916 and 1917 during the Mexican Border crisis. In spite

of various other parallel events and initiatives opposing growth and formalization of the National

Guard, the crisis on the border was a critical event to influence legislation in favor of formalizing

the National Guard as the Regular Army's operational reserve. The crisis took place on the

Southern United States border and escalated dangerously in 1916 to the brink of all-out war

between the United States and Mexico until final resolution in1917. These years were framed by

the somewhat dwindling Mexican Revolution and the rapidly developing events of World War I.

South of the border, the Mexican revolution set conditions for lawlessness and violence which

necessarily and significantly increased the soldier requirements to protect the border. At the same

time across the Atlantic, the Germans were fully engaged in combat operations at the outset of

World War I. While President Woodrow Wilson did not initially believe the United States would

be a participant in the Great War, key military and political leaders, like Theodore Roosevelt and

War Secretary Lindley Garrison, were pushing for an increased preparedness of the United States

military for both protection along the border and fighting capability in Europe should the situation

develop.[1] The angry resignation of Garrison in early 1916 marked the end of legitimate efforts to

dissolve the National Guard in favor of mandatory military service through the "Continental

Army" plan. Garrison's resignation, the objectively purposeful Representative James Hay who

led the Military Affairs Committee, President Wilson's acute knowledge of the potential of

organized militia, the increasing severity of acts associated with World War I, and the immediate

and necessary requirement for more Soldiers along the Southern Border, all combined to define

---

[1] Jim Dan Hill, *The Minute Man in Peace and War: A History of the National Guard* (Harrisburg, PA: The Stackpole Company Telegraph Press, 1964), 226.

the environment in which the National Defense Act of June 3, 1916 came to fruition.[2] The

National Guard officially became the operational reserve of the United States Army.

There is a chronology of events in existing historical accounts regarding the National

Guard when reviewing their role on the border between 1916-1917; various narratives reciting

details but lacking in plot. There is another story to be told that has a plot; and that is the story of

the National Guard, under extremely short time requirements, and still operating under the old

Dick Act of 1903, mobilizing and deploying tens of thousands of troops in support of the

President's directive in order to create conditions on the border that ultimately led to resolution.

President Wilson exercised the new powers under the National Defense Act of 1916 to mobilize

the Guard, but what was the real impetus behind the order? What influences drove Wilson to

issue such a broad directive? A review of the influences will help to uncover the strategic intent

of the mobilization. The purpose of this paper is to examine the role that the National Guard

played in the campaign when called for duty on the Border between 1916 and 1917. This will

help determine their operational impact on the relative success or failure of President Wilson's

strategic aim.

There are volumes of pages filled with the inadequacies, lack of readiness, and inability

of the National Guard to perform their mission in 1916. Many are based on narratives of

personalities, records of complaints, descriptions of discomfort upon arrival, and other matters of

personal interest.[3] These provide insight as to the individual feelings of particular Soldiers, but in

almost all cases do not offer any assessment of the National Guard's collective effect on the

assigned mission. The question that remains after reading any of the literature as a single entity is:

---

[2] Hill, *The Minute Man in Peace and War,* 228. Wilson recognized that it would be much more feasible to expand an already existing force (the organized militia) then to try to man a plan that had to start from scratch.

[3] All the primary source information derived from "official reports" details individual and unit readiness issues. This material was generated by various entities within the War Department and Militia Bureau.

Did the National Guard succeed or fail in their primary assigned mission? As a designated reserve capability, they initially failed the Army's tactical readiness expectations, but in their larger operational role they directly influenced the environment which enabled the president to reach acceptable termination criteria thus ending the armed conflict involving the military. This paper aims to look past the rough surface waters regarding the National Guard's readiness and peer into the depths to find deeper meaning within the operational and strategic context.

It is necessary to go a little further back in history to gain a better understanding of the role, capability, and dynamic of the National Guard. History illustrates tension between the War Department and National Guard, War Department and law makers, War Department and Governors, and in some cases War Department and Executive Branch leadership, like President Wilson.[4] This tension was status quo for the day as is tension in modern day civil-military relations. It is one of the keystone traditions of American government in that the state as an elected representation of its population dictates the mission and makeup of the military in order to ensure their capability to carry out the required tasks associated with national security. It is relevant to outline some of the tensions between the various war department staff, National Guard leadership, congressmen, and other national leaders to understand relevant influences behind the President's decision making. It will also serve to counter the single-sided observations that overtly and subjectively incriminate the Guard's performance without context to causation or explanation. It is not necessary to scope the entire history of the militia which has its origins back to 1636 during which time the settlers of Massachusetts Bay Colony organized themselves in defense of their property. Rather, this paper will reach back in time just far enough, with a brief review of some key legislation and events leading up to the National Defense Act of 1916 and the Guard's subsequent mobilization. The purpose is to illustrate the compressed time frame in

---

[4] Hill, *The Minute Man in Peace and War,* 221.

which the National Guard was given to affect a major shift in structure, personnel, and operational capability that unfolded concurrent to the border crisis. Without at least a brief historical review preceding the Mexican Border conflict, complete understanding of the actual National Guard capability in context to the tactical, operational, and strategic aim is not possible; this is a critical component missing from most primary literature on the topic.

Literature Review

There are generally three groups of literature relating to this topic and time period. First, although within primary sources, narratives by military, political, and civic leaders come up short as an accurate testament as to the impact of the National Guard mobilization. Many previous researchers appear to have depended heavily on these reports and narratives without giving full consideration to the context in which they are associated. The tensions clearly correlate with the discourse between preparedness and non-preparedness political circles and will be addressed in the section regarding a brief history of the National Guard emergence. This review included historical government documents and reports from the period by such members of entities like the War Department, State National Guard Headquarters, Regular Army, Militia Bureau, and General John J. Pershing's own official reports. With the exception of the latter, which focused solely on the punitive expedition into Mexico, these all are similar in that they focus the subject of their reporting on specific information such as numbers of deployable personnel, rifle shortages, and numbers of those needing weapons qualification. Unfortunately they are almost exclusively focused on individual and unit level data rather than how, if at all, the units' collective contributions were linked to termination of the conflict.

The next group of literature cited in this paper is that of secondary sources. They will be referenced for their information drawn from both other original sources and their professional assessments. These historical accounts focus largely on the exciting adventure of Major General John J. Pershing's punitive expedition into Mexico in pursuit of General Francisco Pancho Villa

4

and his semi-organized revolutionary style army of marauders. Retired Colonel Frank Tompkins' book *Chasing Villa* (1934) is a very detailed account of the pursuit of the Villistas. It appears his research is thorough; however, there are two considerations regarding the integrity of the accounts. First, it was not completed until 18 years after the time setting of the incident, and second, Tompkins himself was a topic frequently written about in his own book. He specifically illustrates heroic imagery of the 13th United States Cavalry while under his own command during the years of the Mexican border crisis. [5] While this does not assert a lack of accuracy on the author's part, it provides some understanding of potential bias and lack of detail regarding the National Guard mission. To be fair, Tompkins adds a chapter to the end of his book (the very last chapter seemingly as an afterthought) to discuss the National Guard mobilization. The work does contribute to a broader understanding of the decision making by Generals Frederick Funston and Hugh Scott regarding their evolving concerns about manning and border security. He also boldly asserts, albeit almost in an obsolete small paragraph, that the reason that Mexico did not crush Pershing's expedition and continue on into Texas was a direct and irrefutable result of the rapid deployment of "about 150,000 National Guard troops into the service of the United States for service along the Mexican border […] and when she [Mexico] saw this…had a change of heart and decided to defer the invasion…"[6] Mexico's capability to invade, arguably, was weak by the time the National Guard began massing troops on the border, however, Carranza's posture and rhetoric did not reflect that weakness. Something did indeed change the heart of Mexico and her aggression. That is what Tompkin's gets right. He continues by asserting that President Wilson failed in preventing war in Europe by his decision to not invade in full force into Mexico. Tompkins argues that Wilson's decision weakened our prestige abroad and we lost an opportunity

---

[5] Frank Tompkins, *Chasing Villa* (Harrisburg, PA: The Military Service Publishing Company, 1934). 198.

[6] Tompkins, *Chasing Villa*, 199.

to build the million man army that we would need for World War I.[7] In this opinion he clearly reflected his bias for the Continental Army Plan despite having written the book long after World War I concluded. He misses the point, in retrospect, that had the United States engaged in all-out war with Mexico, it would not have deterred Germany's actions in Europe and would have only served to inhibit the America's capability to enter in the European theater. This would have played perfectly to the German's intent.

In 1969, Clarence Clendenen published his manuscript that centered on the more complex dynamics of the conflict. His *Blood on the Border: The United States Army and the Mexican Irregulars* addressed the gray areas between revolution and organized forces. In his chapter on the mobilization of the National Guard, he uses phrases such as "scraping the bottom of the barrel" in his reference to the Regular Army requiring reinforcements from the militias and Guard.[8] While subjective in his assertions, he is effective in capturing the extreme conditions and time frame in which the mobilization occurred. Clendenen also recognizes the significance of the mass mobilization but misses the opportunity to place it in context to the termination. He instead resorts to drawing the painfully obvious conclusion that the National Guard was more trained and ready after the border deployment than prior.[9] This seems to be the trend among many authors with their assessment of the National Guard.

Arthur Link is well known for his volumes of published studies on Woodrow Wilson. His most useful works for the research of this paper were those that included a compilation of primary

---

[7] Tompkins, *Chasing Villa*, 199.

[8] Clarence C. Clendenen, *Blood on the Border: The United States Army and the Mexican Irregulars* (London: Macmillan Publishing, 1969), 287. He may have been trying to communicate the Army's opinion as seen through their lens. This is not clear though and it casts doubt on the integrity of his unsupported assertions.

[9] Almost every writer who cited the National Guard's role on the border included this common theme. There are no military units that are less trained after a mobilization and deployment than prior, so this recurring point seems wasted and offers nothing with respect to any deeper understanding.

source material.[10] This provided a convenient single source to read Wilson and his staff's correspondence, papers, and letters. Other works were also useful but had to be taken in context with primary source material to balance Link's intense bias for Wilson.[11] Link's material was best for getting an understanding of President Wilson and his policies, but it was clear from his writing that he was a devoted fan of Wilson. Discussion regarding the National Guard was limited to its evolution surrounding the legislative process.

Herbert Mason Junior's *The Great Pursuit* (1970) and Alan Millett's *The General* (1975) are historical accounts that provide different yet useful perspectives. *The Great Pursuit* is useful in the research with its historical accounts of events leading up to the mobilization by illustrating the influence of the German and Austrian advisors to Mexico. It also highlights some of President Wilson's decision making based upon upcoming elections.[12] This will help later in the paper explain the perceived lack of strategic aim. Mason mentions infantry patrols and listening posts but only touches on a larger mission when he states that "more than one hundred and ten thousand national guardsmen were forced to adopt Wilson's old policy of 'watchful waiting.'"[13]

The General recounts the events of retired Colonel Robert L. Bullard's life story that includes his time as a Commander of the combined brigade which was comprised of elements from his old Twenty Sixth Infantry Regiment and three state National Guard units. His force consisted of just over 3,000 Soldiers and was stationed in San Benito.[14] Allan R. Millett, makes the observation that "both the regulars and guardsmen had the gnawing suspicion that the

---

[10] Arthur S. Link and David W. Hirst, eds., *The Papers of Woodrow Wilson, 1916, Vols. 36, 37* (Princeton, NJ: University Press, 1981).

[11] Arthur S. Link, *Wilson: Vols. 4, 5* (Princeton, NJ: Princeton University Press, 1964).

[12] Herbert Molloy Mason Jr., *The Great Pursuit* (New York: Random House, 1970), 218.

[13] Mason, *The Great Pursuit*, 222.

[14] Allan R. Millett, *The General: Robert Bullard and Officership in the United States Army, 1881-1925* (Westport, CT: Greenwood Press, 1975), 287.

mobilization served no immediate strategic purpose."[15] This is the author's opinion through the perceived lens of Bullard derived from primary source correspondence between Generals Tasker Bliss and Hugh Scott. It is a logical opinion but one that lacks real supporting direct evidence. In Millett's book, there is no assertion as to what that strategic purpose was originally, what it should be, or an illustration on Bullard's thoughts on that matter. The topic revolves around his mission to train the Guardsmen in his brigade to an acceptable level of proficiency.

Jerry Cooper's *The Rise of the National Guard* (1997, 2002) is the book of choice to teach West Point students the history of the National Guard. It is a widely accepted standard for accuracy within Army education circles. Cooper provides very direct input as to the reason of the National Guard mobilization. He occasionally uses himself, citing his past research, throughout his accounts of history. Despite his assertion that the Guard was to "patrol the border and deter regular or irregular Mexican forces from crossing," there is no clear citation to any other source to corroborate the assertion.[16] He frankly states in an interview:

> [t]he sentence you quote is mine alone based on conclusions [from] three factors. One: legally and constitutionally, the Guard was the state militia and the Constitution restricted use of the militia to armed service within the United States. President Wilson had no authority to send the Guard into Mexico. Two: the Army viewed the Guard with great skepticism and did not want them involved in their operations on either side of the border. Three: none of the armed services had substantive war plans or mobilization schemes in the modern sense...[17]

While not citing references in the interview correspondence, Cooper still demonstrates an intuitive understanding of the strategic ambiguity of Wilson's foreign policy that oft

---

[15] Millett, *The General,* 288. Demonstrated widespread confusion over the nested mission (tactical mission nested within the strategic end).

[16] Jerry Cooper, *The Rise of the National Guard: The Evolution of the Militia, 1865-1920* (Lincoln and London: University of Nebraska Press, 1997; Nebraska Press, Bison Books, 2002), 159.

[17] Jerry Cooper, interview by author, email, 9 November 2010.

veered from his consistently idealistic rhetoric.[18] His second point captures the tensions

but it simply does not provide answers to the questions for the basis of this paper's

research. The third point is important in that the issue creating difficulties for the Guard

was not the lack of war plans, but instead the lack of substantive war plans. The amended

plans that came from the War College at the request of Scott only addressed the numbers

of personnel required to accomplish a total war intervention. While the operation

depended heavily on a large Guard contingent to reach the necessary manpower

requirement, the plans did not include consideration for the mass mobilization operation.

This aspect of the campaign plan, the needed time and actions to get the Guard from a

Garrison posture into a theater of operation, was lacking. It is in that sense that the war

plans were not substantive.[19]

Intervention (1993), scribed by John S.D. Eisenhower, details the United States Army's

involvement in the Mexican Revolution. Eisenhower includes the period from pre-Carranza

presidency through the withdrawal of Pershing's American forces from Mexico in 1917. He

offers an insightful perspective of the Wilson strategic decision making as influenced by three

false assumptions regarding the perceived operational environment. These false assumptions are

in part the basis of understanding in how Wilson's strategy led to escalation and near war and will

be discussed later in the paper. In this thorough account of the political tension between the two

governments and their respective key actors, Eisenhower unfortunately breezes over the event of

the Guard mobilization, instead choosing to focus on tales of the expedition and colorful vignettes

about Lieutenant George Patton and General Pershing. His only mention of the mission was in

---

[18] Thomas Bruscino, "The Rooseveltian Tradition: Theodore Roosevelt, Woodrow Wilson, and George W. Bush," *White House Studies* 10, Issue 4 (2010).

[19] Hugh Scott to Chief, War College Division, dtd. 16 June 1916, Hugh L. Scott Papers, Box 23 Library of Congress; Copy provided by Dr. Thomas Bruscino, School of Advanced Military Studies, Ft. Leavenworth, KS.

reference to the first deployment of 4,500 soldiers of the National Guard from Arizona, New Mexico, and Texas, and observed that the "border would be less inviting to Mexican depredation."[20] This lack of insight as to the overall mission of the remaining more than one hundred thousand soldiers assigned to the border is a critical shortcoming of his work.

The third and last group of sources for research used in this paper is from National Guard reference material. These are text and references adopted by the Army to study the history of the National Guard. These works have in common a broad sweeping view of history. While Jerry Cooper's last referenced book was used by West Point as a student text, it does not belong with this literature. This group contains work that was formally acquisitioned and given formal military publication title prefixes such as "NGB Pamphlet" and then physically published by the military. Jim Dan Hill's *The Minute Man in Peace and War* attempts to cover the entire history of the National Guard beginning from the first settlers up through 1963. The book was published the next year in 1964. Given the nature of such an endeavor, it is understandable why it does not capture the level of detail necessary in determining the National Guard's relative success, failure, or purpose in its border mission except to observe that the "Regulars and Guardsmen had no immediate military mission....but the force was where the Mexican warlords understood it."[21] In Colonel R. Ernest DuPuy's *The National Guard; A Compact History*, the same history was retold in an even more abbreviated form but offers a sound explanation of the origin of the Stimson Plan which is necessary to discuss in understanding the history of the mobilization of Guard units relevant to this operation.[22]

---

[20]John S. D. Eisenhower, *Intervention! The United States and the Mexican Revolution, 1913-1917* (New York: W.W. Norton & Company, Inc., 1993), 287.

[21] Hill, *The Minute Man in Peace and War,* 233.

[22] Colonel R. Ernest Dupuy, *The National Guard: A Compact History* (New York: Hawthorn Books, Inc., 1971), 94. Describes in general the evolution of Divisions sized units in the Guard.

Michael D. Doubler's *I Am the Guard* reference book (2001) also recounts National Guard history from 1636 through 2000. The same reductionist ambiguity is present in his work, is only slightly more descriptive, and does not reveal any real deeper meaning. An example of this author's description of lessons learned included observations such as, "uniforms, insignia, and unit decorations reflected local, regional, and state pride" and the explanation for mobilizing over more than 110,000 Guardsmen was attributed to the President "fearing a growing crisis."[23] It does, however, offer an excellent desk side reference for the layman who desires a chronology of events that affected the Guard over the course of her history. Elbridge Colby's *The National Guard of the United States; A Half Century of Progress* (1977) is an informative account of the political history of the National Guard evolution. It will be used to cite some political history and illustrate tensions, but does not address the Guard's mission for the border mobilization. It speaks directly to the legislative issues of the day.[24]

During this tumultuous time of history, the identity of the National Guard was consistent: volunteers stepping forward to provide additional wartime capability to ensure the continued security of the American way of life. What was not consistent was the language used to describe the National Guard. This means that some audiences are confused by the varying descriptive terms used to denote National Guardsmen and their units. For example, in Richard Crossland and James Currie's *Twice the Citizen; A History of the United States Army Reserve* (1984), the authors devote much print and space to describing functions of the National Guard although the Guard is not part of the Army Reserve and should not be studied as such.[25] While the historical

---

[23] Michael D. Doubler, *I Am the Guard: A History of the Army National Guard, 1636-2000* (Washington DC: Department of the Army, Pamphlet Number 130-1, 2001), 163.

[24] Elbridge Colby, *The National Guard of the United States: A Half Century of Progress* (Manhattan, KS: Military Affairs / Aerospace Historian (MA/AH) Publishing, 1977), IV.18.

[25] Richard B. Crossland and James T. Currie, *Twice the Citizen: A History of the United States Reserve, 1908-1983* (Washington D.C.: Army Publishing, 1984). Discusses various functions of the Guard throughout entire work, mixing the history of the Guard in with that of the Army Reserve.

review is helpful if studying the National Guard, it presents a deceptive view of what comprises the Army Reserve. Some confusion also lies in modern descriptive terminology which combines National Guard into a larger pool of all military reserve forces referred to as Reserve Component. This is accurate, however Reserve Component should not to be confused or used synonymously with Army Reserve. The Reserve Component label is only most useful when studying macro issues of the military such as end strength and modernization goals. It is certainly not beneficial for this study to regard all Reserve Component entities of that time period as one. To further illustrate the complexity of the language, through the window of time with which the scope of this study will be limited, the following entities existed and are sometimes used interchangeably albeit inaccurately: militia, organized militia, unorganized militia, National Guard, volunteer army, federal reserve force, Continental Army, Officer Reserve Corps, Enlisted Reserve Corps, and state volunteers. Without going into deep discussion on each of these terms and what they represent, discussion will be limited to the following two organizational descriptions which for the studied period are synonymous: the organized militias and the National Guard.

That these secondary sources referenced above lack specific depth regarding the National Guard mobilization and its mission does not preclude them from reference in this research paper. What these sources hold of value is information, that when collectively assembled, will illustrate some commonality in explaining the National Guard's role and effect and help in examining Wilson's policies on the military. Examination of Wilson's policy, illustrating intent, and studying decision making during this conflict is necessary to assert the National Guard's operational purpose in support of the national strategic aim. Then it is fair to make an objective statement regarding success or failure of that campaign.

Methodology

The way in which this paper differs from all other literature on the subject is that it will review and discuss the National Guard's operational mission on the border and its strategic purpose and result. It is to answer the question of why the National Guard was mobilized to the Mexican border and what the mission was that they were to accomplish. But before understanding the mission, the national strategy must be clear. That is to be found within President Wilson's intent together with those in his administration and War Department. When these questions are answered, an objective assessment or assertion can be made with a relatively high value of confidence that the National Guard either succeeded or failed in that mission. The way this paper will answer these questions is to first briefly review the National Guard evolution to the point of mobilization in 1916. Next, the paper will transition into President Wilson's policy and the relevant inputs which influenced his decision making in order to make an assertion as to his strategic aim for the Mexico Border campaign. A review of the military actions leading up to the clear prospect of all-out war will properly frame the problem from the military perspective. The final portion will combine the presidential diplomacy, military operations, and Mexico's perspective. The conclusion will illustrate that despite the National Guard's failure to meet the War Department's expectations for tactical readiness, the Guard's ability to quickly surge forces to the border resulted in a favorable termination of the conflict.

National Guard History in Context to 1916

When the National Guard began arriving on the Mexican Border in 1916, they were still functioning under the Dick Act of 1903, rather than the new National Defense Act of 1916, which had been signed into law just fifteen days earlier. The President was able to exercise his authority to mobilize the militia attributed to incidents of "invasion, insurrection, or threat of invasion."[26] However, they were limited to operations within the continental United States, as the members had not signed new oaths reenlisting themselves into a dual state and federal status. This reality did not stop President Wilson from directing the mobilization of just over 140,000 troops from 47

---

[26] Colby, *The National Guard of the United States*, V.1.

13

states and the District of Columbia.[27] The potential limitation of the Guard's capability to charge south of the border in the event of all-out war did not affect the President's vision on the role they would serve in deploying en masse along the geographic fault line.

President Wilson was a political expert in exploiting tension to turn it into positive political opportunity. Not only could he exploit these opportunities to solidify his own political standing, but more importantly to buy time in order to resolve problems. This he did effectively with the tensions surrounding the evolution of the National Guard who had always contended that they should be the immediate back-up to the Regular Army in order to provide an operational reserve.[28] The state militias were, after all, the only organized reserve component elements. Unfortunately, this idea of state organized readiness to assist the country in areas of national security did not sit well with strong conservative proponents of the preparedness movement. The ability for the organized state militias, with their centralized association which represented them conspicuously in the halls of the legislature, reflected the potential for the country to lean too heavily on this asset and not adequately grow the first line of defense regular force structure. At least this was the perspective of those supporting the preparedness movement.[29] The political landscape at the beginning of the twentieth century included this ongoing discourse. On one side there were those in favor of aggressive preparedness wanting to dissolve the National Guard in favor of a larger Regular Army and Federal Reserves. On the other side were those more aligned with pacifism, neutrality, and non-preparedness. And in the middle was a president who

[27] *Report on Mobilization of the Organized Militia and the National Guard of the United States, 1916* (Washington, DC: Government Printing Office, 1916), 143-144.

[28] Colby, *The National Guard of the United States,* V.4.

[29] Robert K. Wright Jr. and Renee Hylton-Greene, *A Brief History of the Militia and National Guard* (Washington, DC: Departments of the Army and Air Force, Historical Services Branch, Office of Public Affairs, National Guard Bureau, 1986), 26.

recognized the growing crisis in Europe, complications and aggression from Mexico, and most importantly the desire to be re-elected.

The Continental Army Plan was the work of the conservative preparedness proponents and a proposal for a large standing active reserve created in lieu of the National Guard division architecture. It also was created and supported by the Regular Army leaders. The plan advocated conscription and mandatory training in order to fill the extraordinary strength requirements of a 400,000 man standing reserve that would be the Army's first fallback for additional forces.[30] The National Guard saw this initiative as a weakening of their relevance and integrity as it sidelined them as the operational reserve in favor of the standing reserves. Even though Wilson had brought Lindley Garrison in as the Secretary of War under his new administration to replace Henry Stimson, Garrison did not embrace nor support Wilson's political direction with regard to military affairs.[31] As the conflict in Europe escalated, so did the tensions surrounding the preparedness movement. Garrison pushed the Continental Army Plan despite grave differences with civilian lawmakers over its feasibility and acceptability. Although strong language from the President sought to encourage a compromise to the conflict, Garrison was rigidly inflexible in his approach.[32] His differences with James Hay who chaired the Military Affairs Committee arrived at the point in which progress toward a solution was not possible. Citing irreconcilable differences with Wilson policy, Garrison resigned on February 11, 1916.[33] Wilson accepted the

---

[30] Cooper, *The Rise of the National Guard,* 155.

[31] Dupuy, *The National Guard: A Compact History,* 95.

[32] Arthur S. Link, *Wilson: Confusions and Crises, 1915-1916, Vol. 4* (Princeton, NJ: Princeton University Press, 1964), 38-39 .

[33] Lindley M. Garrison Papers, Box 7 Folder 14; Public Policy Papers, Department of Rare Books and Special Collections, Princeton University Library. This collection is stored online at the Mudd Manuscript Library via http://diglib.princeton.edu/ead/getEad?eadid=MC060&kw=#bioghist . Accessed on 10 March 2011.

resignation without reservation and moved forward in finding a solution to placate his constituents.

The president quickly went to work directly with Hay. Wilson recognized the immediate need for growth of the American military capability. He did not, however, intend to separate from all the non-preparedness Democrats that he needed for the upcoming November re-elections. In January 1916, Wilson began his information campaign appealing to both sides of the preparedness conflict. He crafted a theme that was centered on preparing the military to defend the country's peace and honor rather than building a war mongering machine.[34] Despite this paradoxical approach, he was able to remain consistent with his rhetoric in verbally promoting the theme of neutrality, yet accommodated the preparedness movement by acknowledging that growth was necessary in order to protect peace. This created political flexibility in the event any future situation should demand war. The House and Senate went back and forth over the next eight weeks amending the proposals. On June 3, 1916 the National Defense Act was signed into law. This increased the force structure of the National Guard from 100,000 to over 400,000 and doubled the peacetime Regular Army to 175,000 (capable of a war time surge up to 286,000).[35]

The civilian lawmakers had spoken. Their President had listened. From the tensions he had identified a political opportunity. When the dust settled, both poles of the conflict were left dissatisfied; the non-preparedness extremes felt they had been betrayed by their leader. And the preparedness extremists like Theodore Roosevelt and Leonard Wood who had been drafted to lead the effort for conscription were not prepared to give up easily.[36] They had lost their

---

[34] Link, *Wilson: Confusions and Crises*, 46.

[35] Russell F. Weigley, *History of the US Army* (Ann Arbor: University of Michigan Press, 1987), 348.

[36] John Whiteclay Chambers II, *To Raise an Army: The Draft Comes to Modern America* (New York: Free Press, 1987), 104-122. Notes that the preparedness elites sought the help of Wood and Roosevelt to put forward the approach for garnering support.

opportunity to force mandatory military training on the American public through conscription. While the political extremes were disgruntled, President Wilson walked away with a standing organized force of National Guard units numbering close to 200,000 strong that he could quickly mobilize, and a majority of centrist voters who were content with his decisions. This strengthened his position nicely for the upcoming November re-election. It was not the perfect preparedness solution, but it was good enough.

In May 1916, prior to the National Defense Act being signed into law, President Wilson mobilized approximately 4,500 Organized Militiamen in their home states of Arizona, New Mexico, and California to assist with troop shortages. These were intended to supplement the existing Regular Army forces assigned to protect the border and assist with guarding the lines of communication that General Pershing continued to stretch. The farther Pershing went into Mexico, the more infantry regulars he had to pull from the border in order to protect his lines.[37] This initial call for militia mobilization was an immediate response to the tactical deficit General Funston experienced as Pershing pushed into Mexico. This effect will be discussed later in the brief analysis of the military campaign and its influence on President Wilson's decision making process. Wilson approved Funston's request for more troops the day after receiving it, quickly grasping the severity of the immediate situation. Since there was no war ongoing with Mexico, these volunteers were called out for the purpose of "repelling invasion" therefore they were to be kept on soil north of the border.[38] Scarcely a month later, Wilson decided to mobilize about 150,000 volunteers under the organizational division tables that had been introduced by Secretary of War Henry Stimson prior to Garrison's tenure. Despite there being a new law placed into effect fifteen days earlier, Wilson directed the mobilization under the old Militia Act for repelling

---

[37] John B. Wilson, *Maneuver and Firepower: The Evolution of Divisions and Separate Brigades* (Washington, D.C: Center of Military History, 1998), 35.

[38] Cooper, *The Rise of the National Guard,* 158.

invasion to ensure maximum participation of both Organized Militia and those that had begun or already converted to the National Guard units. One can imagine the confusion incurred by the states as they struggled to mobilize old units, new units, and transitioning units under the relatively new division organizational force structure. This confusion and lack of resourcing did not stop states from pushing soldiers as quickly as feasible to mobilization stations and then on to the border.[39]

Even during this tumultuous period of mass mobilization the tensions continued despite having been a final decision and law emplaced regarding the demise of the Continental Army Plan. What evolved was a skewed account of history regarding the National Guard by proponents of that plan who had difficulty or were unwilling to adjust to the idea of the new force structure that was not in concert with their desired vision. When historians take into account the National Guard role in the Mexican Border conflict of 1916, they are inundated by primary sources that focus almost exclusively on the hardships of mobilizing tens of thousands of volunteers, within an organization structure that had not yet fully transitioned, and were needed on short notice. The National Guard had found its legitimacy and in doing so was now going to have to pay the bill. They had evolved this far amidst politically toxic rhetoric, and they would continue to evolve in spite of the overtly negative criticisms. Considering the almost insurmountable request, President Wilson was undaunted in his intent and confident in its desired effect to prevent war with Mexico. He recognized the opportunity that the escalating condition presented. To order the mobilization of all the National Guard divisions and some separate brigades, it is clear he understood that this was the necessary decisive action greatly needed to change the environment in order to conclude the operation on terms favorable to the United States.

---

[39] Clendenon, *Blood on the Border*, 289. The available logistics and transportation support and varying readiness levels of units influenced their time spent at state or regional mobilization stations.

President Wilson's Policy and Strategic Aim

"The chief principle for employment of US Forces is to ensure achievement of the national strategic objectives established by the President through decisive action while concluding operations on terms favorable to the United States."[40] This modern military doctrine, although not codified in 1916, epitomized Wilson's understanding of the necessary conflict termination. It is appropriate to recognize that the ideas of national strategy and strategic or national aim are modern military and political terms and ideas. When used throughout the course of this paper, it is meant to capture the intent of national policy as prescribed by the President and his advisors. It also is used synonymously with the presidential vision for a desirable end to the conflict. Wilson understood the idea of *good enough* in order to adjust focus on the growing conflict in Europe.[41] Jerry Cooper, author of *The Rise of The National Guard*, best captured the idea of national strategy occurring in 1916: [...] there was no such thing as a National Strategic Aim, the term would have been meaningless to all concerned. Historians are divided on what Wilson sought with the intervention [the Pershing Expedition].[42] For historians and researchers alike it is hard to clearly articulate Wilson's strategic aim regarding Mexico. One can only look for consistencies in his spoken intent and applied actions to make an assessment of his strategy. Whether he was undergoing a self-maturation period or reflection and refining, Wilson's actions seemed reactive and to cater to changing reality. Therefore it is much easier to find consistencies in Wilson's policy within small chunks of time. For the purpose of understanding why the National Guard was sent to the border, this paper limits the scope of interest to between late 1915 until the withdrawal of Pershing from Mexico.

---

[40] *Joint Publication 3-0: Operations*, II-1.

[41] Italicized for emphasis; as opposed to *ideal* conditions which may not be congruent with reality.

[42] Jerry Cooper, interviewed by author, 9 November 2010, email.

Wilson was consistent in his message, but his actions over time changed to accommodate the conditions at hand. He appealed to the Democrats and many other voters because of his spoken policies regarding the United States' role internationally. The public depended on him to keep the country out of war, and that idea was a recurring theme in many of his speeches. As Wilson's first term neared its end it became increasingly more important for Wilson to identify with the needs and wants of the public. He first needed, in June 1916, the Democratic nomination for his second term as president. Then he needed to win the election in November 1916. His diplomacy and policy centered on these two needs, but was defined by his ideals of elite morality which influenced inconsistent actions to accommodate ever changing self-revelations with regards to reality.

As the fall of 1915 approached, the commander of the Southern Department, General Frederick Funston, and the Regular Army were unable to maintain protection and security along the Mexican Border despite receiving reinforcements. The numbers were still not adequate to provide the physical coverage required over such a large geographic expanse of terrain. "With the troops so spread out, all they could do was to wait for reports of attacks and try to react as quickly as possible."[43] If the resources were lacking for a strong defense to protect the border, then Funston knew he had to take the offense into Mexico to meet his military objectives. Wilson always preferred, however, to seek diplomatic resolution. While Wilson prevented Funston from sending troops across the border, what did offer temporary reprieve were Wilson's two initiatives in October 1915. The first recognized the de facto military leader, General Venustiuano Carranza as the legitimate governing authority in Mexico and the second allowed Carranza's soldiers to use the American rail to expedite their movements to areas needing immediate security attention. This clever diplomatic move immediately placed Carranza accountable to the United States in a

---

[43] Thomas A. Bruscino Jr., "A Troubled Past: The Army and Security on the Mexican Border, 1915-1917," *Military Review* (July-August 2008), 35.

position by which the President could leverage his diplomatic pressure. It also empowered Carranza with the ways to quickly address the marauders, without excuses, by providing a route to the contested areas near Agua Prieta. Matt Matthews observed in his paper that "[i]n the end, the situation was stabilized, albeit not by the [Regular] Army, but by President Wilson."[44] It was indeed solved by President Wilson, but was by no means the end. It only provided Wilson with a greatly needed temporary reprieve. For Wilson, the factor of time in political diplomacy was of a premium. At the frustration of his military commanders on the border, Wilson had just bought some more time.

If raids into the towns on the American side of the border were the primary concern of the President regarding regional security, then the elements conducting the raids were the center of gravity. What President Wilson addressed with his decisive diplomatic solution was only one actor, Carranza, but still other actors and elements remained and would be have to be addressed as well. The primary entities conducting the raids can be generally and simply grouped by influence and affiliation and viewed over the two year timeframe (1915-1917) as follows:

---

[44] Matt M. Matthews, *The U.S. Army on the Mexican Border: A Historical Perspective* (Fort Leavenworth, KS: Combat Studies Institute Press, 1975), 66.

General Time Frame	Influential Leader	Fighting Forces
Early 1915	Luis de la Rosa Aniceto Pizana	de la Rosa group in relatively small numbers
Summer – Fall 1915	General Carranza de la Rosa	Carranza Officers Soldiers leading or reinforcing de la Rosa with The Plan of San Diego
Spring 1916	Pancho Villa	Aggressive attacks 9 Jan – Train near Chihuahua 8-9 Mar – Columbus, NM
1916	Pancho Villa de la Rosa	de la Rosa taking advantage of Pancho Villa aggressive raids

As a means to illustrate the leadership and groups of the primary influences regarding the physical violence that was occurring along the border, this table is adequate. It does not fully represent the cultural complexities of a country wrought with revolution. It almost implies that the problem facing Funston and his troops was that of organized forces. It is through this lens of simplicity and reduction that Wilson counted on the diplomacy as an effective means to an end through Carranza. This was a source of tension throughout the entire conflict as Wilson's diplomacy and patience directly conflicted with Funston and Pershing's desire to be more proactive in stopping the raids.[45] It also illustrates that, following the recognition of Carranza as the legitimate leader in Mexico, Wilson tackled one problem but left others unaddressed: like Pancho Villa and De la Rosa with his Plan of San Diego. Pancho Villa was Carranza's foe and was infuriated by the U.S. legitimizing Carranza. Additionally, the town of Agua Prieta that was made easily accessible to Carranza by Wilson via rail was also a hub for Villista operations. Villa suffered a humiliating defeat to Carranza at Agua Prieta influenced at least in part by the diplomatic initiative of Wilson. This was especially painful for Pancho Villa as he had been the

---

[45] Bruscino, "A Troubled Past," 34; Funston to War Department, 10 August 1915, *FRUS*-1915, 803.

one lone Mexican supporter of President Wilson during the Vera Cruz intervention.[46] When he

had reconstituted his forces, Villa immediately turned his attention to inflaming the fault line

along the border with well-organized violent raids, and sought to delegitimize Carranza and

demonstrate resolve against President Wilson. The purpose was to invoke revenge on America for

Villa's decisive loss at Agua Prieta and to provoke another intervention to create a "unified

nation" in Mexico.[47]

The problem of the Villa raids was an oversimplified view of the more holistic problem.

President Wilson did not recognize the breadth or depth of the combined problems. He only

recognized the influences as being endemic of the struggling government and Mexican

revolutionary culture. Just as he had reacted to friction with Carranza by addressing that singular

issue, he would attempt to address Pancho Villa in a one dimensional approach as well

overlooking de la Rosa and the Plan of San Diego.

Just a year earlier, Wilson had sent the Navy, Marines and Army into Vera Cruz to unseat

the revolutionary leader Victoriano Huerta. While Wilson's initial attempt was to exercise limited

force to control the wharfs, the Navy and Marines were met with resistance and the entire city of

Vera Cruz had to be occupied. The President did not hesitate in the use of the military as an

extension of his confusing foreign policy practices but was still devastated to hear that American

and Mexican lives were lost.[48] The eventual withdrawal from Vera Cruz was only executed after

a deal was brokered with Carranza to ensure the safety of remaining Americans and Mexicans

who had come under the employment of the Army. Yet after withdrawal Carranza's soldiers

sought retribution on all those same Mexicans. Wilson understood the complexities of the

---

[46] Andrew J. Birtle, *U.S. Army Counterinsurgency and Contingency Operations Doctrine, 1860-1941* (Washington DC: Center of Military History, United States Army, 2004), 199.

[47] Friedrich Katz, *The Life and Times of Pancho Villa* (Stanford, CA: Stanford University Press, 1998), 552-553.

[48] Birtle, *U.S. Army Counterinsurgeny*, 193.

Mexican political and military arena and did not want to get involved in any more interventions. He later articulated this lesson learned in a speech to Congress in 1916 when he requested request to use military force as necessary in Mexico to end the violence.[49] His spoken position during this period consistently reflected a strategic policy in Mexico built on the three following themes:

1) Protecting Mexico's sovereignty (no intervention),

2) Not taking up war with the Mexican people (moral code), and

3) Protecting citizens living in the US from acts of violence and crime (voter interests).

The latter theme was central to his Mexican foreign policy while he embraced the first two in order to avoid war and stay in good graces with the voters for the upcoming election.

As the temporary reprieve from Wilson's diplomacy wore off, March 1916 brought a return of violence unparalleled in previous years. Pancho Villa's raiders attacked Columbus, New Mexico on the night of March 8 to 9 renewing the friction and forcing a decision by key leaders. President Wilson was faced with four potential approaches, other than diplomacy which was now failing, in response to Pancho Villa's raid:

1) Continue the status quo of watchful waiting,

2) Engage in full-scale military intervention,

3) Send the requisite number of reinforcements to protect the border, or

4) Dispatch an expedition in hot pursuit of Villa.

This was an important decision point for the President but one that did not require much thought as, through his lens, they were not really all feasible or acceptable options.

Beginning with the idea of maintaining the status quo and doing nothing, President Wilson viewed this approach as not feasible and certainly not acceptable to his voters and

---

[49] Arthur S. Link and David W. Hirst, eds., *The Papers of Woodrow Wilson, 1916, Vol. 37* (Princeton, NJ: University Press, 1981), 303. From the handwritten draft address to congress scribed June 26, 1916. Wilson wrote, "I am not willing to be a party to intervention in the internal affairs of Mexico."

constituents. He could not embrace a patient "watchful waiting" style of diplomacy as he had with some success in the past.[50] That he was seeking nomination for the Democratic presidential re-election bid was the most obvious reason. He needed to protect the American citizens along the border and demonstrate his political resolve in preventing an escalation which could lead to war. The "White House had been deluged with telegrams from organizations and private citizens pleading for the United States to keep out of war with Mexico; for every wire that advocated further military intervention there were ten strongly against."[51] His intent to avoid war with Mexico was the overarching political rhetoric. But in the hours and days following the Columbus raid, when fickle pressure from his constituency suddenly overwhelmed this theme, he was forced to find a balance between staying out of war and satisfying public sentiment. "Citizen outrage and natural instincts suggested that Villa himself be brought to justice for the attack."[52] After the Columbus raid in March 1916 the public overwhelmingly wanted retribution for Villa. The public wanted to avoid war but now they also sought punishment for Pancho Villa's violent actions against American citizens, and with the upcoming presidential nomination looming over his head, Wilson was not prepared to just watch and wait.

The second approach was intervention; Wilson did not want war with Mexico. There were the very important self-preservation motives for the upcoming nomination and there was also his past experience at Vera Cruz. The idea of intervention also went against two of his repeated points of protecting Mexican sovereignty and not creating war with the people of Mexico. Despite Wilson willingly using it in the past, intervention was an overtly anti-peace theme. He depended on "peace" frequently in speeches to advance his political agenda while

---

[50] Don M. Coerver and Linda B. Hall, *Texas and the Mexican Revolution: A Study in State and National Policy, 1910-1920* (San Antonio:Trinity University Press, 1984), 63.

[51] Mason, *The Great Pursuit*, 218.

[52] Bruscino, "A Troubled Past," 38.

25

keeping in good graces with the pacifist voters. Wilson even used his peace theme as he quietly pushed for an expanded military capability on the platform of "preparedness for preserving peace."[53] It was important for Wilson to keep in good standing with his anti-war political base, even if the rhetoric was just a façade. It was, nonetheless, a consistent façade which proved to be useful in gaining the nomination for his second term. Especially after the Vera Cruz intervention, Wilson was more certain than ever the Mexican population had to work out their differences on their own accord. President Wilson provided his understanding of intervention and its grave effect to Congress, albeit three months after the Columbus raid: "By intervention I mean an attempt to determine for the Mexican people what the form, the circumstances, and the personnel of their government shall be, or upon what terms and in what manner a settlement of their disturbed affairs shall be affected."[54] Regarding this option, it would be impossible to conduct a successful intervention without the full balance the United States' military power available to enter into Mexico. In doing so, Wilson also knew that he would violate the sovereignty of that country.[55] Regardless of the poor ethics and leadership at the federal government level in Mexico, he was committed to avoiding that violation. To compromise the sovereignty would also create undo friction with the Mexican population creating a war with the people.[56] The Army War College further solidified Wilson's assumptions and understanding of an intervention with the following discussion from that same time:

> In an armed intervention it is axiomatic that an overwhelming force used in
> vigorous field operations without costly pauses and directed straight and

---

[53] Link, *Wilson: Confusions and Crises,* 46.

[54] Link and Hirst, eds., *The Papers of Woodrow Wilson,* 303; Draft address to joint session of Congress delivered on June 26, 1916.

[55] Steven T. Ross, *American War Plans, 1890-1939* (London / Portland: Frank Cass Publishing, 2002), 74. Campaign Plan drawn by the War College ten days after the Columbus raid requiring about 250,000 troops to take Northen Mexico with the Navy blockading, while other forces seized Tampico.

[56] Ross, *American War Plans,* 73. "…large elements of the population would resort to guerilla warfare."

continuously at the organized field forces and centers of resources will most effectively and economically overcome organized resistance and make possible a more orderly and more economical period of pacification....To reject these plans, to use only part of the plans, or to curtail the forces outlined in the plans, can but invite local disasters and delays, lengthening the period of military operations, and make more costly in lives and treasure both this period and the period of pacification.[57]

The War College was essentially asserting an all or nothing approach to the use of military force if intervention became a selected course of action. When the Cabinet members issued a notice that "Congress would adopt a resolution calling for armed intervention" in response to the attack on Columbus if the government (President) did not take immediate action, Wilson needed no further persuasion that a limited expedition was necessary. The full armed intervention was exactly what he intended to avoid, and he certainly was not going to accept the risk associated with a limited intervention heeding the warnings of the War College. When presented with the risks for the options that included possible prolonged operations or predictable violation of Mexican sovereignty leading to war with the people, he chose the first. Although Wilson knew of the potential risk of prolonged operations, he thought it more likely that the expedition would be decisive and thus rationalized it would not incur the anger of the population and "could probably be done quickly with a small force."[58]

Third, sending the necessary manpower to the border, as Funston had requested in order to properly secure it and prevent the cross-border incursions, did not appeal to Wilson's reactive style. He already had forces on the border, and there were very few additional available troops to send. The only viable forces remaining were the twelve to sixteen National Guard divisions that stood ready to muster, but the National Defense Act was still not yet signed into Law.

[57] Birtle, *U.S. Army Counterinsurgency,* 202.

[58] Link, *Wilson: Confusions and Crises*, 207. Link does not provide a citation for this assertion of what Wilson "said." However, it is reasonable that Wilson thought the expedition option to be more decisive due to its explicit mission and narrow focus.

Lastly, if Wilson was to commit military action in Mexico in lieu of a congressionally mandated intervention, it needed to be limited. The idea of hot pursuit was diplomatically palatable to Wilson and Baker. Unfortunately, the details of a hot pursuit policy with Mexico were not complete.[59] With Wilson facing nomination for the presidential Democratic bid, the American population furious with Villa, and Congress threatening intervention, he made the only logical decision that would again buy him time and keep the United States out of war while hopefully protecting the sovereignty of Mexico. But in doing so, he completely overlooked the necessity to man the force accordingly. On the night of March 15, 1916, General Pershing pushed across the Mexican Border headed south in pursuit of General Francisco "Pancho" Villa.[60]

Simplified Assumptions, Lack of Guidance

In 1916, Wilson made it clear in speeches to the public that his policy was to stay out of war with Mexico and expand the force capability of the military to adequately defend the nation's peace interests. Yet when it came to border, he left his commanders woefully undermanned, and was now contemplating decisive action with military force into Mexico. His desired state for Mexico was to see Carranza's regulars stabilize the situation in northern Mexico, thus taking responsibility for their side of the border. This would create a safe buffer to protect U.S. citizens and interests. His intent for achieving this state was to *protect* the sovereignty of Mexico, *prevent* waging war with the Mexican population, and *defend* U.S. citizens and Mexicans living north of the border from violence and crime. The only real concrete guidance from this presidential intent was to defend the citizens and Mexicans living north of the border. Even in that capacity he was severely limited under posse comitatus. It was understandably difficult for General Funston, a

---

[59] Link, *Wilson: Confusions and Crises*, 218. As of March 19, Arrendendo and the Secretary of State were haggling back and forth trying to work out the details of such a policy.

[60] Thomas A. Bruscino Jr., "A Troubled Past," 39; Eisenhower, Intervention!, 241.

veteran warfighter with a decorated history and former National Guard Colonel himself, to plan a campaign in these terms.

While military are trained to use force to resolve the problem at hand with the available resources allocated, the position of Funston was further complicated by Wilson's simplified assumptions regarding the environment, human factors, and full scope of the problem. These assumptions led, through rapid escalation in spring and summer 1916, to the near demise of the campaign. Wilson's assumptions included:

> …first of all that Carranza wanted to capture Villa and would therefore render Americans his full and unstinting cooperation. That presupposed that Carranza would allow Pershing to ship men and supplies over the Mexican Northwestern railway. Wilson's third assumption, the most unrealistic of all, was that the Mexican people in the region would be eager to help capture Villa.[61]

Pancho Villa, however, was not the only cause of the border violence in 1916. The Plan of San Diego under the lead of Luis del la Rosa was a source of past, present, and future violence that was entangled directly and indirectly in the Carranza military establishment.[62]

The War Department sent word to General Funston that he have General Pershing go into Mexico with a designated unit to track down the attackers from the Columbus raid and then withdraw after being relieved by Carranza's soldiers. The desired tactical end state for this course of action was that "Villa's band or bands [were] known to be broken up."[63] The expedition was intended by Wilson and Baker to be a shaping operation to support the main effort of protecting the border. From an operational perspective, however, the main effort was not resourced properly to effect success. To the commanders the expedition must have appeared as the only option in

---

[61] John S. D. Eisenhower, *Intervention!* 236.

[62] Randolph Robertson (Vice Counsul), Report on Plan of Sand Diego to Secretary of State, June 9, 1916, *Papers Relating to the Foreign Relations of the United States* (Washington D.C.: Government Printing Office, 1925), 570-572.

[63] Link, *Wilson: Confusions and Crises*, 208. Link provides excerpt from primary source correspondence from The Adjutant General to the Commanding General, Southern Department (Funston), March 10, 1916, State Department Papers.

which to get at the perceived threat with military force given there was no additional manning provided to fill the void that was left along the border. As the War Secretary pointed out later, "The expedition was in no sense punitive, but rather defensive."[64] To clarify this after the conflict is representative of the confusing guidance the Southern Department faced from the State Department, the War Department, and the President.[65] The idea of the expedition being punitive may have been propagated by Baker himself when he requested Scott to draw up the orders for assembly of a punitive expedition.[66] Punitive or otherwise, it did not matter to Wilson. What was important for his purposes was that the voters were satiated and that it would immediately arrest the problem at hand.

It is not clear if Wilson was certain the expedition would solve his Mexico problems. It is certain that he needed it to maintain the political initiative both for the elections and with his diplomatic efforts with Carranza. The other point was that he did not offer a clear vision to his commanders on how the expedition would end. That would be his most dangerous simple assumption: that the expedition would be quick, small, and need only limited force.

Challenging Campaign

When General Pershing launched his expedition into Mexico, it was the critical juncture at which the military operation began to diverge from the Wilson political rhetoric. If Wilson's desired state was to end violence along the border in order to protect American lives and interests in the region (with a sub plot of gaining votes for the next election), it is difficult to explain how he thought Pershing's expedition could accomplish that end unless he viewed Villa as the sole problem as previously addressed.

---

[64] James A. Sandos, "Pancho Villa and American Security," 310. References primary source correspondence between H.L. Scott to L. Wood, March 11, 1916, Scott Papers.

[65] Tompkins, *Chasing Villa*, 72. State Dept. press release describing the single purpose to capture Villa. War Dept. ordered Pershing to pursue and disperse.

[66] Link, *Wilson: Confusions and Crises*, 208.

The border campaign had begun to suffer prior to the Pershing expedition, before there were tangible signs of tactical complication and indications of operational culmination. Through the winter of 1915, Funston's campaign was doing little other than enjoying a relatively short reprieve from Villa's raids and de la Rosa's Plan of San Diego. Without permission to cross the border and kill or capture raiders, his 20,000 soldiers were forced into a dispersed defense. This averaged about ten men per mile if all were stretched out defending at once along the nearly 2,000 miles.[67] Given the alternative choice of sitting on the border and waiting for the enemy to attack in a location not protected, Funston and his subordinate commanders were eager for a chance to get at the root cause of the problem.

The idea of Wilson not fully understanding the environment, which led to an incomplete understanding of the problem, left General Funston with only bad choices. With too few forces to adequately defend the border, Funston was drawn into pattern recognition from the past lessons learned, and wanted to mass his forces for a decisive action against Villa's forces.[68] "If we fritter away the whole command guarding towns, ranches, and railroads, it will accomplish nothing if he [raiders] can find refuge across the line."[69] Funston clearly believed that the Army "should play a more aggressive role in stopping the raids."[70] The raid in Columbus, New Mexico on the night of March 8, 1916 by Pancho Villa's band of outlaws was exactly the catastrophic result Funston had been expecting. He was ready to push his Army forces immediately into Mexico. Within six days,

---

[67] Eisenhower, *Intervention!*, 211. It is not clear the specific date this strength applies although Eisenhower does reference "latter half of 1915" later in the paragraph. It was certainly prior to 1916.

[68] Daniel R. Beaver. *Newton D. Baker and the American War Effort, 1917-1919* (Lincoln: University of Nebraska Press, 1966), 17. Funston had two feasible options, mass troops on the border in sufficient number to accomplish the mission, or take the balance forward to secure Northern Mexico by force.

[69] Matt M. Matthews, *The U.S. on the Mexican Border: A Historical Perspective*, 67. Cited from "General Funston to the Adjutant General, March 10, 1916," Papers Relating to the Foreign Relations of the United States With the Address to the United States of Congress, December 5, 1916, University of Wisconsin Digital Collection, 482-483; Tompkins, *Chasing Villa*, 70.

[70] Bruscino, "A Troubled Past," 34.

that is exactly what he did. After receiving the directive, Funston sent Pershing across the border on the night of March 15, 1916 with about 4,800 troops.[71] Pancho Villa's band was ordered broken up until the Carrancistas could take the mission over and keep the raiders in check in Northern Mexico.[72]

By avoiding the full-scale intervention and not immediately mobilizing the necessary forces to properly secure the border, Wilson unwittingly created a larger problem centered on the personnel shortages which led to escalating tensions with Mexico. First, the expedition aggravated the shortage of troops. Maneuver operations consume more personnel. The longer the operational reach of the maneuvering elements, the more troops are required to prevent culmination. Funston pushed available troops to assist Pershing, and later in May 1916, Wilson accommodated Funston's request for about 4,500 Guardsmen.[73] Had the proposed Continental Plan, calling for 400,000 reservists to serve six years on duty instead of the already existing 130,000 National Guardsmen, to perform duty as the primary operational reserve of the Army, it would have taken years to reach that level of training and proficiency.[74]

Secondly, the length of those supply lines created undue tactical risk. Not only did Pershing have to figure out how to man the logistical trains, he had to protect those critical supplies. Because of the personnel shortages, Pershing had to accept unusual tactical risk with sparsely protected lines.[75] As Pershing moved further into Mexico in pursuit of Pancho Villa, the lines of communications became increasingly more spread out and vulnerable to disruption. The

---

[71] Ross, *American War Plans,* 74.

[72] Tompkins, *Chasing Villa,* 70-71.

[73] *Report on Mobilization of the Organized Militia and the National Guard of the United States, 1916,* 10. Newton Baker directed the mobilization of NM, AZ, and TX "for the proper protection of that frontier."

[74] Steven Weingartner, ed., *Cantigny at Seventy-Five: A Professional Discussion* (Chicago, IL: Robert R. McCormick Tribune Foundation, 1994), 39.

[75] Don M. Coerver, "Mexican Border Battles and Skirmishes," *The War of 1898 and U.S. Interventions, 1898-1934* (New York/London: Garland Publishing, Inc., 1994), 324.

longer the lines of communication the more regulars that were required to push and defend the logistics into Mexico and the less that were available to defend the border. It was an operational catch twenty-two. By mid-April, the logistical support for Pershing's expedition became so intensive that the number of troops required to guard and move supplies consumed more than what was needed at the front of the long line.[76] To mitigate the risk to Pershing, Funston opened an additional line of communication requiring even more troops on April 12. On the same day Major Frank Tompkins, whose unit was short rations as a result of the obtuse operational reach, attempted to resupply in the town of Parral. While there, he and his troops were subjected to an armed and angry mob of Mexican civilians who began throwing rocks and chasing him and his men. About 300 Carrancistas joined the affray and continued the pursuit of Tompkins' unit. In the ensuing skirmish, Tompkins along with five others was wounded and two were killed.[77] If ever Funston and Pershing had an opportunity to evaluate the nested effect of the expedition on their campaign plan, this was it. But the moment and its key indicators illustrating potential war with the population and the growing necessity of the Carrancistas to protect Mexico's sovereignty was missed or ignored and simply slipped past.

Lastly, the personnel requirements of the maneuver elements were drawn from the border. Pershing's expedition created a protection void in certain areas along the border increasing the opportunity for attack as troops were pulled from the border to protect the lines and provide logistical support inside Mexico.[78] In today's doctrinal terms, the tactical mission behind the Pershing expedition was to attack and destroy Pancho Villa and his forces in order to protect the Americans along the border by rendering the raiding parties incapable (or in the case of their specific order – dispersed). However, if unable to accomplish the mission objectives quickly, this

---

[76] Link, *Wilson: Confusions and Crises*, 280.

[77] Tompkins, *Chasing Villa*, 137-139.

[78] Coerver and Hall, *Texas and the Mexican Revolution,* 100.

operation would become extremely vulnerable. As Pershing's expedition grew, it necessarily drew resources away from the border, and opened vulnerabilities in the vicinity of key municipal nodes just inside the United States. The border immediately become more porous and this set into motion an escalation of violence and friction which would lead the conflict down a path to war.

These three components of the problem were ultimately the foundation for a reverse in progress towards peace along the border in the early spring of 1916. The skills of the Regular Army, their past experience, or the creative genius of their commanders could not overcome the inherent battlefield friction incurred by such an overwhelming geographic disadvantage aggravated by too few soldiers.

An Intervention by Any Other Name…

Pershing was a battle focused commander who was not intent on losing. He pushed so fast and so far that his mission erroneously became the supported operation. At the beginning of March 1916, with strength now of 6,675 troops strong and 350 miles deep in a sovereign nation, reality displayed a building of combat power inside Mexico and positioning of those combat forces for offensive operations.[79] At least that is what must have been perceived by Carranza, the Carrancistas, and the people of Mexico with whom Wilson did not wish to wage war.

While Pershing had some tactical success, his effort more accurately distracted Pancho Villa while the expedition deteriorated and became part of the strategic problem rather than the tactical solution. Meanwhile, Funston allowed the expedition to become the main effort. There was really little other choice. Pershing and his forces became a critical vulnerability and the lines supplying him a critical requirement. With every day passing, the problem became worse. Within four short weeks, with Pancho Villa on the run but still at large, the border was scarcely defended,

---

[79] Link, *Wilson: Confusion and Crises*, 217. Troop strength and distance into Mexico.

and Pershing began to culminate. This was precisely the vulnerability that de la Rosa could exploit to reincarnate the Plan of San Diego in a reinvigorated effort.

De la Rosa believed that the trouble with Villa offered an opportunity to renew his efforts, so he began reconstituting his force. He and several other Mexican leaders reorganized the military wing of the Plan of San Diego. For a time this force worked with elements of the Carranza government to threaten the United States with invasion as a method for driving out Pershing's force.[80] The Plan of San Diego was under way and sought the opportunities created by Pershing and his troops moving away from the border. The criminal elements that were participating in the raids concurrently to Pancho Villa were very likely many of the same Mexican rebels who actively supported the Plan of San Diego. And many of these were, while loyal to the new Mexican government, likely led or assisted, supported, and even influenced in some part by officers acting on direction from the Carranza staff.[81] Because of this complex relationship and Wilson's failure to recognize those relationships the decision to ultimately send Pershing's expedition south exacerbated the already difficult force structure challenges.[82] While Villa was certainly a force to be reckoned with, there were other viable influences and forces to fill the void created as he and his men drained resources from the unprotected border.

After the Tompkins skirmish with the population and Carrancistas at Parral, Pershing requested even more troops. As a military leader, Pershing embraced lethality and was intent on crushing his opponent. Except now Pershing had shifted his focus to Carranza and his regulars. He felt the threat had changed to that of the Mexican Army more so than that of Villa and stated

---

[80] Bruscino, "A Troubled Past," 39.

[81] Louis Ray Sadler, e-mail correspondence to author, December 11, 2010. Addresses direct relationship between Carranza government and Plan of San Diego.

[82] Bruscino, "A Troubled Past," 33. Federal and Army officials' confusion regarding recognition of the depth of the problem.

as much in a press release declaring the Villa chase "on hold."[83] The request was honored and

Funston dispatched two additional regiments to Namiguipa on April 18.[84] Funston and Scott

realized the gravity of the situation and decided to pull Pershing back in order to concentrate his

forces vicinity Colonia-Dublan and reconstitute. The operational approach of sending General

Pershing in after Pancho Villa had now come to serve the exact opposite of the purpose the

expedition had intended. It had some successful encounters against Villa's men, but Villa was

still at large. The personnel void had created an irreversible vulnerability on the border.

Sovereignty had been defended by Carrancista regulars and it was hard to argue no violation of

sovereignty when Pershing's force was numbering close to 10,000. The population had become

angry with the occupation and turned against Tompkins in a violent rage. And finally, diplomacy

now centered on withdrawal of the expedition rather than finding a solution to the security

problems in northern Mexico. It had become the primary source of the friction rather than a

means to help overcome that friction. Conditions were getting worse, but Wilson was not making

any decisions in reaction to the changing environment. Funston was left to figure out how to

protect Pershing's columns and also defend the border.

Deteriorating Situation

The situation deteriorated even further when on May 6, the renewed Plan of San Diego

raiders attacked Glen Springs and Boquillas, Texas. A mini expedition from the Eighth and

Fourteenth Cavalry under Colonel Frederick W. Sibley promptly assumed command from Major

George T. Langhorne, who did not intend to pursue the raiders.

> Lack of transportation and properly defended lines of communication preclude
> any extended pursuit into Mexico and military men here do not think another
> punitive expedition possible because of the lack of cavalrymen. [...T]here are no

---

[83] *New York Times*, "Pershing Halts," written April 18, 1916, published April 21, 1916.

[84] Link, *Wilson: Confusions and Crises*, 284.

more troops of cavalrymen that we can draw on. [...] We simply have not the men for another expedition.[85]

Despite the shortages, Sibley gave chase and pursued the perpetrators 180 miles deep into Mexico before returning to the United States.[86] It appeared that Villa and Carrancista forces had joined their efforts in order to attack north of the border. Raiders shouted both "Viva Villa" and "Viva Carranza" during the raid.[87] Carranza, probably inflamed as a result of the Sibley expedition, alerted his northern Mexico commanders to the threat of potential war. Naturally, this event precipitated the immediate need for more American troops. Generals Funston and Scott sent a request to the War Department which was immediately approved with the dispatch of 4,000 Regular Army soldiers. President Wilson also saw fit to mobilize the first wave of organized militia. He called the border states of Texas, Arizona, and New Mexico into service on May 9, 1916 which mustered between 3,000 to 4,500 troops.[88] Nine days later Carranza sent another alert, this time in the form of a directive, to his commanders at Nueva Laredo and Matamoros, to fight any of Funston's forces that crossed the border. He also notified the governors and commanders in northern Mexico to prepare for war.[89] On May 19, Funston sent word to Pershing and warned him of the impending buildup of Carrancista troops in northern Mexico. To Funston, this sudden build up, despite it being exactly what the diplomatic efforts had been intending to achieve, seemed dangerously suspect.[90] When Carranza's forces finally began movement into

---

[85] *New York Times*, "Langhorne Leads Pursuit," May 9, 1916, querynytimes.com.

[86] Link, *Wilson: Confusion and Crises*, 291.

[87] Eisenhower, *Intervention!* 286.

[88] *Report on Mobilization of the Organized Militia and the National Guard of the United States, 1916*, 10.

[89] Link, *Wilson: Confusion and Crises,* 296. Citing Carranza's telegrams to various generals. Also correspondence from Consul in Tampico and Frontera to the Secretary of State on 13 and 16 May, 1916.

[90] Link, *Wilson: Confusion and Crises,* 297. Quoting Funston to Pershing, May 19, 1916, State Department Papers.

northern Mexico, it was not carried out under the conditions that Wilson had visualized. Funston recognized this and his warning to Pershing reflected this useful assessment of the conditions.

Bruscino notes in his article, "A Troubled Past," "The issue of border security dominated the diplomatic discussions between the United States and Mexico, so much that the withdrawal of the punitive expedition became predicated on the stabilization of the border."[91] While there is merit to this observation, it would be equally accurate to state that through the lens of Carranza, the punitive expedition dominated the diplomatic discussions, and that the security on the border became predicated on removal of the expedition. On May 18 General Jacinto Trevino deployed 15,000 troops and 26 trains from Saltillo headed north, followed about two weeks later by a terse ultimatum from Carranza to Wilson: Remove Pershing's expedition from Mexico or she would be forced to defend her sovereignty against the invaders.[92] It was again a clear indication that the diplomatic efforts had been inverted by Wilson's flawed approach to sending in Pershing's expedition without the requisite forces to sustain the operation and protect the border. By the middle of June the situation had become so dire that Wilson and Baker sent what amounted to the last available 1,600 Regular Army troops to join the effort. Following this deployment, there were little if any available manning resources remaining that were not committed to the Southern Department on the border. Despite the added forces, another Plan of San Diego raid near San Ignacio attacked a border patrol unit wounding seven and killing three. Trevino warned Pershing that any movement of columns other than north out of the country would be engaged. While this exchange occurred, Mexico called all males in Ciudad Juarez to colors and issued guns to citizens in Nuevo Laredo.[93]

---

[91] Bruscino, "A Troubled Past," 41. This quotation specifically addresses post mobilization conditions, however the diplomatic conditions as he describes were present in May and June 1916 as well.

[92] Link, *Confusion and Crises,* 297. Quoting Douglas to Luis Cabrera, telegram, May 27, 1916, Polk Papers, who was reporting on a conversation with Secretary Lansing.

[93] *New York Times*, June 17, 1916; Link, *Wilson, Confusions and Crises*, 300.

The situation deteriorated to such a state that although neither side at the national political level wanted war, all came to except that it was likely unavoidable. Scott responded by directing the War College Division to prepare a war plan for invasion, protection of the border, and protection of American property and interests in Mexico, as was standard protocol for the day.[94] The War College had created several such war plans but they were much more specific to the need for full scale intervention by means of an invasion driving all the way to Mexico City. These plans were recommended to, but for the most part not exercised by, Wilson.[95] The personnel requirements made the plans not feasible and as mentioned earlier President Wilson was trying to get out of the intervention business in Mexico that he had gotten into two years prior. Endeavors with such a scope would be a sure depletion of critical resources required in the event the United States had to enter the war in Europe.

It is not apparent from reading accounts by Pershing of his own mission that Wilson had made any effort to communicate a strategic intent through Funston to the tactical commander.[96] He had sent four points of order on the day Pershing was launching across the border, but like much of Wilson's input it was vague in military terms. Any commander would have a difficult time with guidance that included "[u]pon no account…shall this expedition…be given the appearance of being hostile…to the dignity of Mexico." What does that mean in terms of military force getting at the root cause of a problem? Wilson had made the decision to send the expedition, but he had not synchronized it with the required sustainment operation and border protection. Thus Wilson did not empower his military leaders and subsequently positioned them for ultimate

---

[94] Hugh Scott to Chief, War College Division, June 16, 1916, Hugh Scott Papers, Box 23, Library of Congress; copy provided by Dr. Thomas Bruscino, School of Advanced Military Studies, Ft. Leavenworth, KS.

[95] Ross, *American War Plans*, 69-75.

[96] MG John. J. Pershing, *Punitive Expedition Report*. Never addresses options or recommendations or how to use the expedition to create conditions that might leverage diplomacy. Reports were tactics centric, omitting considerations of the larger operational campaign or strategic aim of the President.

failure on the operational scale. Although progress had been forged by distracting Villa and thus keeping him from the border until at least June, Wilson now fought to mitigate the presence of Pershing's expedition while on the very cusp of all-out war. The regular forces available alone would not bring Wilson's mess to a close. For Wilson, time could solve most problems or at least allow them to solve themselves. With the probability of war looming in Europe, however, Wilson was out of time and men. He had to bring the conflict to an end. On June 18, 1916 Wilson called out the full balance of the Organized Militia and National Guard divisions amounting to 140,016 troops and sent them in a mass mobilization through their states' deployment stations and to the border.[97]

National Guard Mission and Impact

In a report from the War Department and Militia Bureau submitted by Brigadier General William A. Mann, Chief of the Militia Bureau, he detailed in one of the most comprehensive and intricate records the chronological data, strength numbers, training status, and mobilization locations of the National Guard's role in the conflict, up until the point of discussing the operational or strategic impact. Within this 169 page report covering the mobilization, only a page and a half is dedicated to the actual mission on the border. It skips discussion of the collective mission requirements, capability, or desired conditions for termination, and overlooks the Guard's role in those desired conditions. One useful sentence can be gleaned from the report; "The mobilization was the outcome of a national emergency demanding extra military service beyond that which could be furnished by the Regular Army... The Regular Army on the Mexican border could be [reinforced] no other way."[98]

---

[97] *Report on Mobilization of the Organized Militia and the National Guard of the United States, 1916,* 143-144.

[98] *Report on Mobilization of the Organized Militia and the National Guard of the United States, 1916,* 5.

Other official reports reflect biases that are difficult to ignore. One example is *The Mobilization of the National Guard, 1916* which was scribed by the Executive Committee of the Mayor's (of New York) Committee on National Defense. It is a summary of an inquiry conducted, as disclosed in the conclusion, to make recommendation for the "need [...] for a standing army sufficient for the protection of the country's borders..."[99] So while it contains some useful information on economic impact to National Guard families, local businesses, and the city of New York, it fails to address the issue of mission success and or purpose. Its real intent is revealed in the conclusion as it displays the bias for a standing Continental Army. This is typical of many reports of the day. The argument and initiatives by most of the Army for a large Continental Army did not end with the formalization of the National Guard after the National Defense Act became law. It continued through the months and years following, and is evident in the numerous reports by Army entities from that era.

Some reports and official accounts go a little deeper by discussing the mobilization of the National Guard in order to protect railroads and other utilities on the Mexican Border and also train in the "mobilization camps since war with the German Imperial Government" had begun.[100] Topics relating to the latter part of this insight might encourage some to argue that the impending American involvement in World War I was the root cause for the 1916 mobilization, and the border violence just an opportunity to validate the Guard. This idea is akin to a test, audit, or grand preparedness inspection to gauge the readiness of the country's reserve military. There is simply no evidence found in conducting the research for this paper supporting this overzealous assertion. However, as it became clearer to President Wilson that the United States was indeed

---

[99] *Report of the Executive Committee of the Mayor's Committee on National Defense. The Mobilization of the National Guard, 1916: Its Economic and Military Aspects.* By Willard Straight, Chairman (New York: 1917), 10.

[100] Annual Reports of the War Department. *Report of the Chief of The Militia Bureau Relative to The National Guard of The United States: 1917* (Washington Government Printing Office, 1917), 12.

going to commit forces in the Great War, then decisions were made on manning regarding recently mobilized units and retaining them for service abroad, which explains historical accounts like the one above.[101] It still does not explain the intended strategic aim of sending the National Guard to the border. There are other works as well, like from the Missouri Military Council's account of that particular state's mobilization through the compilation in 1934 of records and reports from the dates of execution. It only reports names of officers and soldiers who participated in the mobilization. It also traces the locations of their regiment en route to Laredo, Texas and the speed in which they mobilized. [102] These reports all have in common a narrative chronicling the order of events and locations, but they also have in common a lack of deeper meaning or description of how this mobilization was nested in the war department's strategic or even the regional operational end state. How, if at all, did the National Guard's mobilization contribute to the ultimate successful outcome in the state of affairs along the border?

There are small discrepancies in accounts of the National Guard's mission on the border between 1916 and 1917. By most all accounts, authors repeat the assertion that the National Guard did not cross the border into Mexico. This is logical, as they had been mobilized under the 1903 Militia Act and were to stay north of the border to prevent invasion. The only author discovered in this research to assert that National Guard Soldiers crossed the Rio Grande with Pershing's expedition was Clarence Clendenon in *Blood on the Border*. He consents that no organic units crossed the border but some "individuals from these two regiments, however, crossed the border on various duties."[103] Lastly, Pershing's own very thorough personal report on the expedition, dated October 10, 1916 makes absolutely no mention of any militia or Guard units

---

[101] Matthews, *The U.S. on the Mexican Border: A Historical Perspective*. 69.

[102] Missouri National Guard, Military Council. *History of the Missouri National Guard* (Missouri Military Council Publishing, 1934).

[103] Clendenon, *Blood on the Border*, 296. In reference to Soldiers from the 1st New Mexico Infantry, and the 2nd Massachusetts Infantry.

or service members participating in his operation in Mexico.[104] His report includes detailed after action reviews and summaries of various staff entities and subordinate units. It also strengthens the stated assumption by other authors that no Guard units operated south of the border. In determining how the Guard was collectively utilized in the operational and strategic role, the paper will keep to the idea that the units did not travel south of the border.

Some units were able to expedite their movement to the border while others were held up at their state or regional mobilization centers. With the National Defense Act having become law only fifteen days earlier it is a remarkable event that units and personnel were even able to initiate movement without getting bogged down in bureaucracy and logistical barriers. The sense of urgency regarding national security and a will to succeed proved to be the National Guard's greatest strength to overcome the friction. Despite the seemingly overwhelming challenges, disorganization, and lack of planning by the War Department, by the end of June "60,000 men on the border in one month accomplished what four months…" had failed to do.[105]

> …the concentration of national guard on the border brought a prompt return of peaceful conditions. To the Mexicans it must have appeared a considerable army. Raids ceased. There was no need for the president to draft the national guard into the federal army under the new defense law and it served throughout the call under which it could have been used only to 'repel invasion.'[106]

The Guardsmen were unable to successfully mobilize as organic divisions, due to primarily two conditions: their peace time strength requirements only requiring about two-thirds their war-time strength and the ongoing reorganization to the actual division force structure. Yet, by July 31, 1916 about "112,000 Guardsmen were in place along the border" with a roll call of

---

[104] Pershing, *Punitive Expedition Report.* Following examination of entire report.

[105] Marvin, "Marking Time with Mexico," 526.

[106] Ward Schrantz, *Guarding the Border: The Military Memoirs of Ward Schrantz, 1912-1917,* Jeff Patrick, ed. (College Station: Texas A&M University Press, 2009), 98.

158,664 who had reported when called.[107] A strong signal of American resolve had been sent and Carranza recognized it. As early as June 23, Carranza had influenced a cessation of violence among the Plan of San Diego perpetrators. While he did not maintain complete control over the organization, his influence ran deep. By July, the "raiding under the Plan of San Diego had run its course."[108] The National Guardsmen had set to guarding railroads, bridges, key infrastructure, towns, and conducting security patrols on the north side of the border. Their duties included sandbagging fortifications at strategic points along the Rio Grande and manning listening posts along the river.[109] They were not tactically capable of conducting collective combat operations. But they were perfectly capable of conducting security operations to protect the border. They also set out to train and improve their war fighting skills. All those opportunities were just a bonus from the perspective of the mission. Most importantly, they had succeeded in shifting the main effort back to that of protecting the border. This dynamic shift immediately changed the conditions which resulted in an environment that created opportunities. Opportunity for Wilson to do what he tended to do best – react. With the violence in Northern Mexico coming into check, Wilson offered to Carranza to push the remaining conflict issues to a Mexican-American Joint High Commission in July 1916. Pershing remained in Colonia-Dublan but with a much smaller force and was restricted from conducting any deep raids. This measure once again bought Wilson the valuable time he needed. This time it was to get through the presidential campaign for reelection. The Joint High Commission had its fair share of tension, but it was mostly relegated to the commission, only occasionally requiring input from the President and Carranza. Pancho Villa began a renewed effort but it stayed within Mexico. As far as proactive military leaders go, as late as December 1916, Funston and Pershing still offered plans to Baker and Wilson for a major

---

[107] Wright and Hylton-Greene, *A Brief History of the Militia and National Guard*, 28.

[108] Clendenen, *Blood on the Border*, 106.

[109] Mason, *The Great Pursuit,* 222.

offensive to Durango to catch Pancho Villa.[110] Prudently, Wilson ignored this offer and focused

his effort on ending the Mexican Border crisis on terms favorable to the United States (which was

leaning heavily towards WWI). By January 1917, General Francisco Murguia delivered a

smashing defeat to Villa at Jiminez, Wilson made a firm decision to withdraw Pershing, the Joint

High Commission ratified the protocol, and on February 5, 1917 the last of Pershing's troops

were out of Mexico. [111] Shortly thereafter, National Guard soldiers began their redeployments and

preparation for entry into World War I.

Conclusion

From the end of 1915 until 1917, President Wilson articulated consistent rhetoric

regarding his approach to stay out of war with Mexico in order to win the election. It was to

protect her sovereignty, avoid creating war with the people, and protect the American citizens

living along the border. Despite strong military and political tension throughout 1916 regarding

the preparedness movement, he catered politically to the pacifists. He, however, was no pacifist.

Wilson recognized the need to grow the capability of the military but approached the topic of the

Continental Army with extreme caution. Opposed to mandatory military training and peacetime

conscription, Wilson ensured that the military did not bully the lawmakers into an obese

Continental Army Plan or the proposed million-man army. He instead accepted the

recommendation of his federal lawmakers and opted for legitimizing the National Guard as a

potential federal force in times of national emergency. That action was accelerated as a need for

more forces on the border loomed ahead. It was good enough.

The War Department and Militia Bureau had done little to modernize the Guard, and

preparedness movement leaders like Theodore Roosevelt and Leonard Wood cast them in a

---

[110] Link, *Wilson: Campaigns for Progressivism and Peace: 1916-1917, Vol. 5* (Princeton, NJ: University Press, 1964), 328-333.

[111] Eisenhower, *Intervention*, 307.

negative light. Military leaders believed there was no reason for the Continental Army Plan to not succeed. However, in the light of the upcoming presidential election and a nation that was largely anti-war, Wilson signed the National Defense Act into legislation on June 3, 1916. The timing was critical. Wilson's self-centric political ambitions, his inability or unwillingness to read the environment accurately, and the Southern Military Department's proactive approach to executing a full military solution to the perceived problem had led the United States and Mexico to the brink of all-out war.

The National Guard was Wilson's last resort for averting war with Mexico, and on June 18, 1916 he mobilized the entire twelve division force structure of the new National Guard. Within days, Carranza changed his position and used his influence to impact cessation of the Plan of San Diego raids. He had de la Rosa arrested and Carranza's regulars began an aggressive campaign against Villa. The operational capability to mobilize more than 150,000 troops with no prior planning, coordination, or real support spoke volumes about the American will to persevere in the face of extreme diversity. The mobilization marked the operational turning point that changed the dynamics of the campaign enabling the effective mobile defense. Most importantly, in combination with Pershing's force on stand-by in Colonia-Dublan, it was the strategic advantage Wilson needed to take back the diplomatic initiative.

This campaign represents a borderline failure attributed to bad national policy fortunately transformed into strategic victory. Victory was not decisive in conventional terms, and therefore cannot be measured in terms of battles won or lost. The United States did not annihilate the enemy. Pershing's expedition failed their tactical mission and did not achieve their stated objective: to capture or kill Pancho Villa. The National Guard was not collectively trained and ready to fight as divisions as had been outlined. And the expedition failed their tactical objective to protect the border from raids. All as a result of a misguided President and administration who failed to commit their efforts to a properly identified problem. When there seemed no other recourse but all-out war with Mexico, despite these setbacks, the President and his military leadership were able to conceive an ending through decisive action, by quickly massing the National Guard on the border, in order to conclude operations on terms favorable to the United States. And this, as President Wilson and his staff clearly understood it, was good enough.

APPENDIX A Reference Timeline

- **Early 1914**: Wilson obsessed with the notion of ousting Victoriano Huerta. "I am going to teach the South American republics to elect good men!" Intervention strategy in effect.

- Provided 10,000 rifles to Venustiano Carranza's men

- **9 Apr 1914**: Huerta's soldiers arrested several American sailors in the port of Tampico.

- **21 Apr 1914**: US Marines seize the wharves at Vera Cruz then the entire city after meeting resistance. 130 US dead / several hundred Mexicans dead.

- **30 Apr 1914**: Funston relieves the Navy in Vera Cruz with 4000 soldiers, and joined the remaining 3000 Marines placing them all under Funston's command.

- **Mid-Jul 1914**: President Huerta resigns from Presidency

- **9 Nov 1914**: Carranza issue blanket amnesty to all Amercanistas who worked for the Army during the American occupation of Vera Cruz.

- **23 Nov 1914**: U.S. withdraw from Vera Cruz

- **15 Jan 1915**: Sherriff discovers document on Brasilio Ramos about The Plan of San Diego

- **April 1915**: Villa is defeated in Matamoros and Celaya by Carranza

- **May 1915**: Raids into Texas increase sharply

- **May – July 1915**: de la Rosa and Pizana, increase acts of violence during raids with the de la Rosa Gang and Plan of San Diego

- **Early August 1915**: de la Rosa, assisted by Carranzistas Officers, raid the King Ranch

- **8 Aug 1915**: Ranger and vigilante TX law enforcement groups kill 102-300 Mexicans and Mexican Americans in response to King Ranch raid.

- **August to September 1915**: Regular Army (Funston and Bullard) failing security mission

- **14 October 1915**: Wilson grants Carranza soldiers use of American railroads to get through Laredo and Eagle Pass

- **19 October 1915**: Wilson recognizes Carranza as the legitimate head of government

- **21 October 1915**: Raids temporarily cease as a result of Wilson's diplomatic initiatives, but now Villa is extremely discontented

- **8 to 9 Mar 1916**: Villa attacks the town of Columbus

- **10 Mar 1916**: Wilson orders Funston to organize a pursuit expedition to capture Villa and preventing any further raids.

- **16 Mar 1916**:1230 AM General Pershing crosses border into Mexico with the initial expedition.

- **17 Mar 1916**: Pershing arrived at the Casas Grandes-Colonia Dublan complex.

- **20-21 Mar 1916:** Carracistas attack Villa at Namiquipa.

- **25 Mar 1916**: Wilson makes public statement reaffirming the intent of the expedition was to capture Pancho Villa – not an invasion of Mexico.

- **26 Mar 1916:** Villa breaks through Carrancista lines and continues retreat to Guerrero.

- **28 Mar 1916:** Villa attacks Guerrero and destroys 172 Carrancistas stationed there.

- **29 Mar 1916:** COL Dodd meets Villa at Guerrero and drives him into retreat.

- **29 Mar 1916:** Villas Chief Commander GEN Elisio Hernandez is killed by COL Dodd's troops.

- **1 Apr 1916:** COL Brown intercepts Villa in retreat vicinity Bachiniva. Villa is wounded in the leg but successfully retreats toward Parral. 30 Villistas dead.

- **10 Apr 1916**: Pershing begins to culminate. His operational reach is at its limit. Funston is unable to continue getting supplies to the very front. The lines of communication are so stretched, that all the forces required to guard it are consuming all the supplies traveling down the line.

- **10 Apr 1916**: At Pershing's request, Funston opens another line of communication and sends more troops into Mexico.

- **12 Apr 1916**: MAJ Frank Tompkins attempts to purchase rations in Parral. He and his 100 CAV Troops are chased from the town by the angry and an additional 300 Carrancistas. Tompkins and 5 of his troops were wounded; 2 killed.

- **17 Apr 1916**: General Leonard Wood and Former President Theodore Roosevelt openly criticize the Hay/Chamberlain Army Reorg Bill as a public safety menace, foolish, and unpatriotic.

- **17 Apr 1916**: Angry about the incident at Parral – Pershing recommends to the War Department what is essentially an all-out war.

- **17 Apr 1916**: Pershing requests two more regiments (INF and CAV).

- **18 Apr 1916**: Two requested regiments are dispatched to Columbus then moved to Namiquipa.

- **18 Apr 1916**: Pershing bypasses formal channels and releases his own press statement accusing Carrancistas of a premeditated attack at Parral and recommending seizure of Chihuahua. Also said he was no longer focused on Pancho Villa, but now reorienting his attention to the Carrancista regulars as they were deemed a greater threat.

- **18 Apr 1916**: Wilson's signs the Hay/Chamberlain Bill into law (published in the NDA as Army Reorg.)

- **22 Apr 1916**: Scott and Funston agree they need to pull Pershing back and have him concentrate his forces to reconstitute vicinity Colonia-Dublan.

- **5-6 May 1916**: Plan de San Diego Raiders hit Glen Springs and Boquillas, TX.

- **7 May 1916**: The Sibley expedition pushes 180 miles deep into Mexico following raids at Glen Springs and Boquillas.

- **7 May 1916**: Sibley expedition incriminates diplomacy effort and Carranza threatens to treat future expeditions as invaders.

- **8 May 1916**: Carranza sends war warnings to all his commanders in Northern Mexico.

- **9 May 1916**: Scott and Funston offer to gradually withdraw the Pershing Expedition to Namiquipa and then farther northward if the President was convinced that the Mexican Government was capable of protecting the border.

- **9 May 1916**: Wilson mobilizes about 4,500 organized militia (National Guard) from AZ, NM, and TX, and an additional 4000 Regular Army. Funston requested them as a precaution.

- **11 May 1916**: Wilson reiterates his two deeply seated convictions: 1) should not be another predatory enterprise like the war with Mexico, and 2) Citizens of Mexico have the right to do as they damn well please w/ their own affairs (non-intervention). (Link)

- **18 May 1916**: Carranza orders forces at Nueva Laredo and Matamoros to fight any U.S. forces that crossed the border. He reinforced his war cry for any and all Governor's and Commanders in Northern Mexico to prepare for war.

- **19 May 1916**: Funston warns Pershing about the massive Mexican troop movements to the north. Realizing that Carranza appears to be accommodating the U.S. request to secure the Northern

Region, but suspecting the quantities as staging for combat with U.S. forces. Prepares contingency instructions for Pershing in the event Pershing is attacked.

- **20 May 1916**: General Trevino deploys from Saltillo and heads to the border with 15,000 troops and 26 trains.

- **31 May 1916**: Carranza states the ultimatum clearly to the U.S.: Withdraw the expedition or Mexico will defend itself from the invaders. If the mission was to disperse Villa as Wilson had originally reassured, then that had been accomplished. Yet the expedition was still in Mexico with no apparent intent of withdrawing.

- **3 Jun 1916**: National Defense Act of 1916 – Legitimizes the National Guard as the primary operational reserve to the Regular Army.

- **12 Jun 1916**: War Department sends another 1600 (Regular Army) troops to the border.

- **15 Jun 1916**: Mexican Irregulars (Plan de San Diego) cross the border near San Ignacio and attack a border patrol unit wounding 7 and killing 3 U.S. troops.

- **16 Jun 1916**: Pershing inflames the friction by responding to a warning from General Trevino that should Pershing try to move any direction other than north, he will be engaged by Mexican regulars.

- **16 Jun 1916**: Scott directs the War College Division to prepare a War Plan that addresses: 1) protecting the border, invasion along the rail lines of communication, and 3) protects American property and interests in Mexico.

- **16 Jun 1916**: Mexican Government calls all males in Ciudad Juarez to colors, and issues guns to citizens in Nuevo Laredo.

- **17 Jun 1916**: 400 US CAV cross into Mexico in response to the attack on 15 Jun, only to return a day later.

- **18 Jun 1916**: Mexican Forces fire on a Navy landing party from USS Annapolis in Mazatlan harbor killing 1 and wounding several other sailors.

- **18 Jun 1916**: 125,000 – 140,000 National Guard mobilized.

- **21 Jun 1916**: Pershing's troops attacked by Carrancistas at Carrizal. 22 US / 30 Mex. casualties.

BIBLIOGRAPHY

Baker, Ray Stannard. Woodrow Wilson: Life and Letters; Facing War, 1915-1917. New York: Doubleday, Doran and Company, Inc., 1937.

Bartlett, Ruhl J., ed. *The Record of American Diplomacy: Documents and Readings in the History of American Foreign Relations.* "President Wilson's Warning on the Danger of War," Address at Pittsburgh, January 29, 1916. House Document No. 803, 64th Congress, 1st Session, Vol. 144 (7098), "Essential Terms of Peace," from *Papers Relating to the Foreign Relations of the United States,* 1917, Vol. I. "President Wilson's War Message," February 3, 1917, 65th Congress, 1st Session, Vol. 55, Part I. New York: Alfred A Knopf, Inc. Third Ed. 1954. Previous ed. 1947, 1950.

Birtle, Andrew J. U.*S. Army Counterinsurgency and Contingency Operations Doctrine, 1860-1941.* Washington DC: Center of Military History, United States Army, 2004.

Bruscino, Thomas A. Jr. "A Troubled Past: The Army and Security on the Mexican Border, 1915-1917." *Military Review* (July – August 2008): 31-44.

Bruscino, Thomas. "The Rooseveltian Tradition: Theodore Roosevelt, Woodrow Wilson, and George W. Bush." *White House Studies 10, Issue 4* (2010).

Chambers, John Whiteclay II. *To Raise an Army: The Draft Comes to Modern America.* New York: Free Press, 1987.

Clendenon, Clarence C. *Blood on the Border: The United States Army and the Mexican Irregulars.* London: Macmillan, 1969.

Coerver, Don M. "Mexican Border Battles and Skirmishes." *The War of 1898 and U.S. Interventions, 1898-1934.* New York/London: Garland Publishing, Inc., 1994.

Coerver, Don M. and Linda B. Hall. *Texas and the Mexican Revolution: A Study in State and National Border Policy, 1910 1920.* San Antonio, TX: Trinity University Press, 1984.

Colby, Elbridge. *The National Guard of the United States: A Half Century of Progress.* Manhattan, KS: Military Affairs / Aerospace Historian (MA/AH) Publishing, 1977.

Cooper, Jerry. *The Rise of the National Guard: The Evolution of the Militia, 1865-1920.* Lincoln and London: University of Nebraska Press, 1997. Paperback Reprint, Nebraska Press, Bison Books, 2002.

Crossland, Richard B. and James T. Currie. *Twice the Citizen: A History of the United States Army Reserve, 1908-1983.* Washington DC: Office of the Chief, Army Reserve, 1984.

Doubler, Michael D. *I am the Guard: A History of the Army National Guard, 1636-2000.* Washington DC: Department of the Army, Pamphlet Number 130-1, 2001.

Dupuy, Colonel R. Ernest. *The National Guard: A Compact History.* New York: Hawthorn Books, Inc., 1971.

Eisenhower, John S. D. *Intervention!: The United States and the Mexican Revolution, 1913-1917.* New York: W.W. Norton & Company, Inc., 1993. Paperback Reprint, 1995.

Lindley M. Garrison Papers, Box 7 Folder 14; Public Policy Papers, Department of Rare Books and Special Collections, Princeton University Library. This collection is stored onsite at the Mudd Manuscript Library via http://diglib.princeton.edu/ead/getEad?eadid=MC060&kw=#bioghist . Accessed on 10 March 2011.

Hill, Jim Dan. *The Minute Man in Peace and War: A History of the National Guard.* With a foreword by George Fielding Elliot. Harrisburg, PA: The Stackpole Company Telegraph Press, 1964.

Jones, Vincent C. "Chapter 16; Transition and Change, 1902-1917," *American Military History.* Publications from the Army Historical Series, ed. Office of the Chief of Military History. Washington, D.C., 1956. Reprint 1989. Database on-line. Available from Center of Military History Digital Archives. Page updated 27 April 2001.

Katz, Friedrich. *The Life and Times of Pancho Villa.* Stanford, CA: Stanford University Press, 1998), 552-553.

Link, Arthur S. and David W. Hirst, eds. *The Papers of Woodrow Wilson.* Vols. 35-37, *1916.* Princeton, NJ: Princeton University Press, 1980.

Link, Arthur S. *Wilson: Confusions and Crises: 1915-1916, Vol. 4.* Princeton, NJ: Princeton University Press, 1964.

Link, Arthur S. *Wilson: Campaigns for Progressivism and Peace: 1916-1917, Vol. 5.* Princeton, NJ: Princeton University Press, 1965.

MacDonald, Charles B. "Chapter 17; World War I: The First Three Years," in *American Military History.* Publications from the Army Historical Series, ed. Office of the Chief of Military History. Washington, D.C., 1956. Reprint 1989. Database on-line. Available from Center of Military History Digital Archives. Page updated 27 April 2001.

Marvin, George. "Marking Time with Mexico: Why the National Guard was Unprepared to Guard the Nation." *World's Work* 32 (September 1916): 526-533.

Mason, Herbert Molloy Jr. *The Great Pursuit.* New York: Random House, 1970.

Matthews, Matt M. *The U.S. Army on the Mexican Border: A Historical Perspective.* Fort Leavenworth, KS: Combat Studies Institute Press, 1975.

Millet, Allan R. The *General: Robert Bullard and Officership in the United States Army, 1881-1925.* Westport, CT: Greenwood Press, 1975.

Missouri National Guard, Military Council. *History of the Missouri National Guard.* Missouri: Military Council Publishing, 1934.

"Mobilization in Spite of War Department," *National Guard Magazine,* Vol. 13. Aug 1916.

Pershing, MG John J. *Punitive Expedition Report.* Colonia Dublin, Mexico: October 10, 1916.

Pogue, Forrest C. *George C. Marshall: Education of a General. 1880-1939.* With a foreword by General Omar N. Bradley. New York: The Viking Press, Inc., 1963. Reprint, New York: Penguin Books, Ltd., 1993.

Report of the Executive Committee of the Mayor's Committee on National Defense. *The Mobilization of the National Guard, 1916; Its Economic and Military Aspects.* By Willard Straight, chairman. New York: 1917.

Report of the Chief of the Militia Bureau; Relative to The National Guard of the United States. Washington D.C.: Washington Printing Office, 1917.

Report on Mobilization of the Organized Militia and the National Guard of the United States, 1916.

Ross, Steven T. *American War Plans, 1890-1939*. Portland and London: Frank Cass publishers, 2002.

Sandos James A. "Pancho Villa and American Security: Woodrow Wilson's Mexican Diplomacy Reconsidered." *Journal of Latin American Studies 13, No. 2* (November 1981).

Schrantz, Ward L. *Guarding the Border: The Military Memoirs of Ward Schrantz, 1912-1917*. Canseco-Keck History Series, ed. Jeff Patrick, no. 13. College Station: Texas A&M University Press, 2009.

Scott, James B. *The Militia, Extracts from the Journals and Debates of the Federal Convention, the State Contitutional Conventios, the Congress, the Federalist, together with Other Papers Relating to the Militia of the United States.* Senate Public Document No. 695, 64th Congress, 2nd Session. Washington, D.C.: 1917.

Schlesinger, Arthur Meier and Francis Lee Higginson. *The Rise of Modern America; 1865-1951*. New York: MacMillan Company, 1925. Reprints: 1933, 1941, and 1951.

Tompkins, Frank (COL). *Chasing Villa*. Harrisburg, PA: The Military Service Publishing Company, 1934.

Weingartner, Steven, ed. *Cantigny at Seventy-Five; A Professional Discussion: Session One*. Chairman: Harold Nelson in Wheaton, Illinois. May 28-29, 1993. Participants: Robert A. Doughty, Jerry Cooper, Edward M Coffman, Douglas V. Johnson, I.B. Holley Jr., Lee Kennett, John T. Nelson II, Robert D. Ramsey III, and Dale E. Wilson. Chicago: Robert McCormick Tribune Foundation, 1994.

Weigley, Russell F. *History of the US Army*. Ann Arbor: University of Michigan Press, 1987.

Wilson, John B. *Maneuver and Firepower; The Evolution of Divisions and Separate Brigades*. Publications of the Army Lineage Series, ed. Jeffrey J. Clark, CMH Pub. 60-14. Washington, D.C: 1998. Database on-line. Available from Center of Military History Digital Archives.

Wright, Captain Robert K. Jr. and Renee Hylton-Greene. *A Brief History of the Militia and the National Guard*. Washington, DC: Departments of the Army and Air Force, Historical Services Branch, Office of Public Affairs, National Guard Bureau, 1986.

Made in the USA
Lexington, KY
27 January 2017